WASHINGTON FOOTBALL TEAM

ALL-TIME GREATS

BY TED COLEMAN

Book design by Jake Slavik
Cover design by Jake Slavik

Photographs ©: Daniel Kucin Jr./AP Images, cover (top), 1 (top); David Durochik/AP Images, cover (bottom), 1 (bottom); Bettmann/Getty Images, 4; Focus on Sport/Getty Images, 6; Tony Tomsic/Getty Images Sport Classic/Getty Images, 9; Ronald C. Modra/Getty Images Sport/Getty Images, 10; Focus on Sport/Getty Images Sport/Getty Images, 12; Shawn Thew/AFP/Getty Images, 14; Scott Cunningham/Getty Images Sport/Getty Images, 16; Doug Pensinger/Getty Images Sport/Getty Images, 18; G Fiume/Getty Images Sport/Getty Images, 20; Rey Del Rio/Getty Images Sport/Getty Images, 21

Press Box Books, an imprint of Press Room Editions.

ISBN
978-1-63494-434-2 (library bound)
978-1-63494-451-9 (paperback)
978-1-63494-484-7 (epub)
978-1-63494-468-7 (hosted ebook)

Library of Congress Control Number: 2021916620

Distributed by North Star Editions, Inc.
2297 Waters Drive
Mendota Heights, MN 55120
www.northstareditions.com

Printed in the United States of America
012022

ABOUT THE AUTHOR

Ted Coleman is a sportswriter who lives in Louisville, Kentucky, with his trusty Affenpinscher, Chloe.

TABLE OF CONTENTS

CHAPTER 1

THE EARLY YEARS 5

CHAPTER 2

SUPER BOWL GLORY 11

CHAPTER 3

THE MODERN ERA 17

TIMELINE 22

TEAM FACTS 23

MORE INFORMATION 23

GLOSSARY 24

INDEX 24

BAUGH

33

CHAPTER 1

THE EARLY YEARS

The Washington Football Team began playing in 1932. Back then, the team was based in Boston, Massachusetts. In 1937, the franchise moved south to Washington, DC. The team became instant champions in the nation's capital. **Sammy Baugh** led Washington to the National Football League (NFL) title that season. The team won another title in 1942.

Baugh could do it all. On offense, he was a star quarterback. On defense, he recorded 31 career interceptions. He was also one of the best punters in football. When the Hall of Fame

was created in 1963, Baugh was one of its first members.

Washington lost the NFL championship game in 1945. After that, the team struggled for years. But things started to improve in the 1960s. That's when **Sonny Jurgensen** took over as quarterback. His strong arm and risky style gave fans plenty to cheer for. Jurgensen led the NFL in passing yards three times while playing for Washington.

Jurgensen had two great receivers. **Bobby Mitchell** was one of the first Black players to play for Washington. Mitchell had incredible speed. In both 1962 and 1963, he led the NFL in receiving yards.

In 1964, Mitchell was joined by **Charley Taylor**. Taylor started his career as a running back. But after a few years, he switched to wide receiver. Taylor still holds the team record for most touchdown catches.

STAT SPOTLIGHT

CAREER TOUCHDOWN CATCHES

WASHINGTON FOOTBALL TEAM RECORD

Charley Taylor: 79

Linebacker **Chris Hanburger** joined Washington in 1965. He rarely missed a game during his 14 years with the team. No other Washington player has matched Hanburger's nine Pro Bowl appearances.

By the early 1970s, Washington had many veteran players on the team. In fact, fans called them the "Over the Hill Gang." All that experience paid off. In the 1972 season, Washington made it all the way to the Super Bowl.

CHANGING THE NAME

When the Washington Football Team formed in 1932, they were known as the Boston Braves. A year later, they changed their name to the Boston Redskins. They kept the Redskins name when they moved to Washington in 1937. Over the years, many people said the name was racist. In 2020, the team's owner finally agreed to change it. The franchise started calling itself the Washington Football Team. The team planned to announce a new name in 2022.

Running back **Larry Brown** led the team in rushing that season. He also scored 12 touchdowns. Unfortunately for Washington fans, Brown couldn't find a way to score in the Super Bowl. The Miami Dolphins won 14–7.

Safety **Ken Houston** came to Washington in 1973. He seemed to know where passes were going before the quarterback did. Houston grabbed 24 interceptions during his time with the team.

THEISMANN
7

CHAPTER 2
SUPER BOWL GLORY

Quarterback **Joe Theismann** took over as the team's starter in the late 1970s. It wasn't long before he led Washington to new heights. In the 1982 season, Theismann helped the team win its first Super Bowl. He tossed two touchdown passes in the game. Washington beat the Miami Dolphins 27–17.

Theismann won 77 games during his 12 years with the team. No other Washington quarterback has won more than 52. Theismann also became the top passer in franchise history. He set a team record with 25,206 career passing yards.

During the Super Bowl, Miami had no answer for **John Riggins**. The bruising running back exploded for 166 yards in the game. His rumbling 43-yard touchdown early in the fourth quarter gave Washington the lead.

Washington made it back to the Super Bowl the next season. However, the team lost to the

Los Angeles Raiders. Washington returned to the Super Bowl in the 1987 season. This time, the franchise scored a Super Bowl–record 35 points in a single quarter. Washington crushed the Denver Broncos 42–10.

Receivers **Gary Clark** and **Art Monk** helped carry that Washington team. And they were both still with the franchise in 1991. That season, Washington won yet another Super Bowl. Clark had 114 receiving yards in the game. Monk wasn't far behind, with 113. Monk spent a total of 14 years with Washington. During that time, he hauled in a team-record 888 catches.

THE HOGS

Washington had one of the best offensive lines in football during the 1980s. They also had a colorful nickname. Center Jeff Bostic, guards Russ Grimm and Mark May, and tackles Joe Jacoby and George Starke were known as the Hogs. To honor the Hogs, some fans still wear pig noses to games.

A great defense helped make Washington's success possible. Defensive tackle **Dave Butz** was the captain of the first two Super Bowl teams. Meanwhile, **Dexter Manley** was a punishing defensive end. When Manley left

Washington, his 97 sacks were a team record. He teamed up with **Charles Mann** to form a fierce pass rush. Mann had 10 or more sacks in four different seasons.

Linebacker **Monte Coleman** spent his entire career with Washington. He was a key member of all three Super Bowl teams. Coleman racked up more than 1,000 tackles during his 16-year career.

Cornerback **Darrell Green** was drafted in 1983. He stayed with the team all the way through the 2002 season. During his incredible 20-year career, Green intercepted 54 passes. He returned six of them for touchdowns.

STAT SPOTLIGHT

CAREER GAMES PLAYED

WASHINGTON FOOTBALL TEAM RECORD

Darrell Green: 295

LACHEY

79

CHAPTER 3

THE MODERN ERA

Joe Gibbs served as Washington's head coach for all three Super Bowl wins. He was one of the greatest coaches in NFL history. However, Gibbs retired after the 1992 season. And without Gibbs leading the team, Washington struggled for much of the next three decades. Even so, fans had no shortage of great players to watch.

Left tackle **Jim Lachey** joined the team in 1988. He carried on the Hog tradition. Lachey made the Pro Bowl twice during his time with Washington.

Running back **Brian Mitchell** was one of the NFL's best-ever return men. In his 10 seasons with Washington, he returned seven punts and two kickoffs for touchdowns. Mitchell never ran for more than 311 yards in any season. Still, he made the Pro Bowl in 1995.

The Hog tradition continued when **Chris Samuels** joined Washington in 2000. The hulking left tackle made six Pro Bowls in his 10 seasons with the team.

Running behind Samuels was a flashy back named **Clinton Portis**. Portis spent only seven seasons in Washington. Even so, he is second in team history with 6,824 rushing yards. In 2005, he broke the team's single-season rushing record. He ran for 1,516 yards that season. His mark stood for seven seasons.

REPLACING A LEGEND

From 1981 to 1992, **Joe Gibbs** won 124 games as Washington's head coach. After he retired, the franchise struggled to find a replacement. The team brought in some big names over the years. They included Marty Schottenheimer and Steve Spurrier. However, none of them found a way to make it back to the Super Bowl. Gibbs returned as Washington's coach in 2004. By that time, the magic was gone. Gibbs went 30–34 in four seasons.

After Samuels retired, Washington moved on to its next great offensive lineman. **Trent Williams** spent nine years leading the latest edition of the Hogs. He was named to the Pro Bowl seven years in a row during his time with the team.

Even with great players like Williams, Washington made the playoffs only twice in the 2010s. In 2020, Washington hired veteran head coach Ron Rivera. He led a team with good young players back to the playoffs.

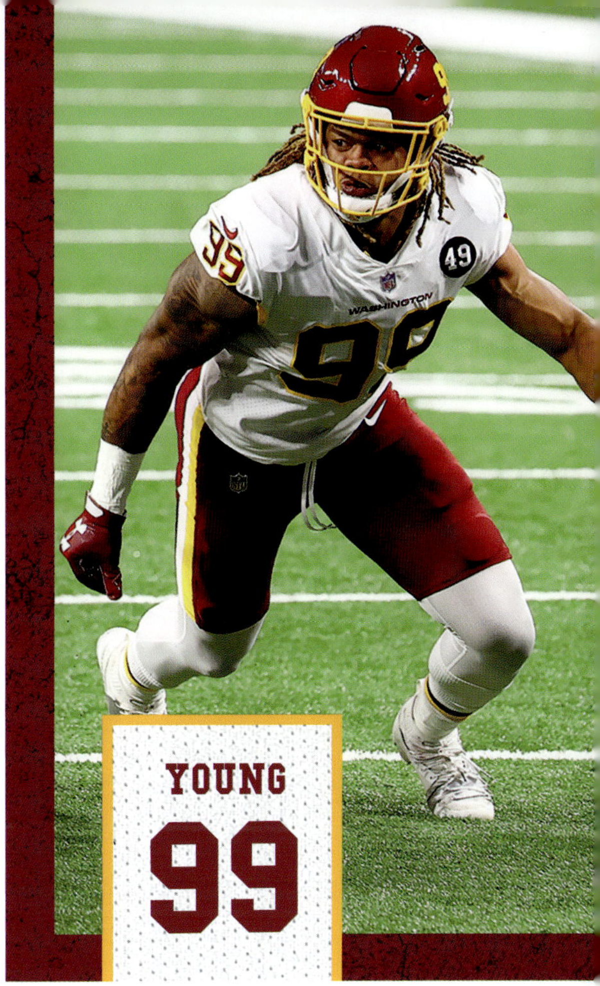

One of those bright young stars was defensive end **Chase Young**. Young won Defensive Rookie of the Year in 2020. He recorded 7.5 sacks and forced four fumbles that season. Rivera loved Young's leadership so much that he named him captain late in the year. Washington fans hoped Young would lead the team for many years to come.

TIMELINE

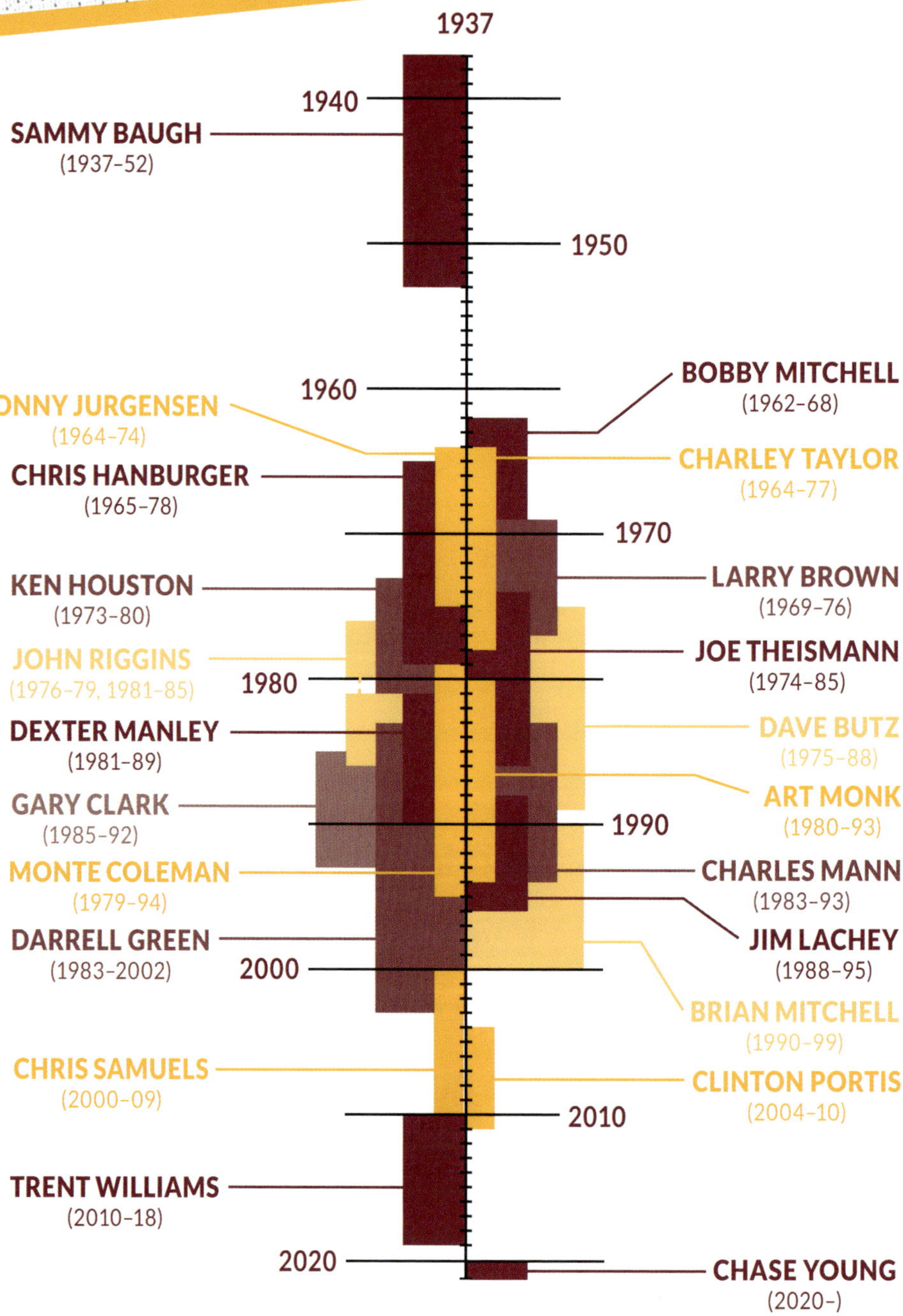

1937
1940
SAMMY BAUGH
(1937–52)
1950
1960
BOBBY MITCHELL
(1962–68)
SONNY JURGENSEN
(1964–74)
CHARLEY TAYLOR
(1964–77)
CHRIS HANBURGER
(1965–78)
1970
KEN HOUSTON
(1973–80)
LARRY BROWN
(1969–76)
JOHN RIGGINS
(1976–79, 1981–85)
JOE THEISMANN
(1974–85)
1980
DEXTER MANLEY
(1981–89)
DAVE BUTZ
(1975–88)
GARY CLARK
(1985–92)
ART MONK
(1980–93)
1990
MONTE COLEMAN
(1979–94)
CHARLES MANN
(1983–93)
DARRELL GREEN
(1983–2002)
JIM LACHEY
(1988–95)
2000
BRIAN MITCHELL
(1990–99)
CHRIS SAMUELS
(2000–09)
CLINTON PORTIS
(2004–10)
2010
TRENT WILLIAMS
(2010–18)
2020
CHASE YOUNG
(2020–)

To Caleb and Abby, the future is bright.

Lerner Publications Company
An imprint of Lerner Publishing Group, Inc.
241 First Avenue North
Minneapolis, MN 55401 USA

For reading levels and more information, look up this title at www.lernerbooks.com.

Main body text set in Albany Std. Typeface provided by Agfa.

Library of Congress Cataloging-in-Publication Data

Names: Hill, Anne E., 1974– author.
Title: A'ja Wilson / Anne E. Hill.
Description: Minneapolis: Lerner Publications, [2022] | Includes bibliographical references and index. | Audience: Ages: 7–11 | Audience: Grades: 2–3 | Summary: "Las Vegas Aces power forward A'ja Wilson is a two-time WNBA All-Star. Discover how this MVP stays in shape, see how she performs on the court, and learn more about her life outside of basketball"—Provided by publisher.
Identifiers: LCCN 2021000089 (print) | LCCN 2021000090 (ebook) | ISBN 9781728436623 (library binding) | ISBN 9781728436630 (paperback) | ISBN 9781728436647 (ebook)
Subjects: LCSH: Wilson, A'ja, 1996– —Juvenile literature. | Women basketball players—United States—Biography—Juvenile literature. | African American women—United States—Biography—Juvenile literature.
Classification: LCC GV884.W67 A6 2022 (print) | LCC GV884.W67 (ebook) | DDC 796.323092 [B]—dc23

LC record available at https://lccn.loc.gov/2021000089
LC ebook record available at https://lccn.loc.gov/2021000090

Manufactured in the United States of America
1-49627-49557-4/13/2021

Lerner SPORTS

SPORTS ALL-STARS

A'JA WILSON

Anne E. Hill

Lerner Publications ◆ Minneapolis

Wilson has her eyes set on the Olympic Games. Due to COVID-19, the 2020 Summer Olympics was postponed. But when the next Summer Olympics takes place, Wilson and the talented US team will be ready to bring home gold. Wilson feels honored to play for her country. Her future is bright both on and off the court.

Wilson keeps her hands on the ball during a USA Basketball Women's National Team game.

All-Star Stats

The 2020 WNBA season marked Wilson's third year in the league. She was already the leading scorer on her team. That season she became one of the leading scorers in the league. Compare Wilson's offense to the WNBA's other top scorers in 2020.

Player	Points	Points per game
1. Arike Ogunbowale	501	22.8
2. A'ja Wilson	450	20.5
3. DeWanna Bonner	434	19.7
4. Breanna Stewart	394	19.7
5. Kelsey Mitchell	394	17.9
6. Skylar Diggins-Smith	390	17.7
7. Betnijah Laney	378	17.2
8. Myisha Hines-Allen	374	17.0
9. Diana Taurasi	356	18.7
10. Napheesa Collier	355	16.1

Glossary

app: software designed for a specific purpose that can be used on a phone or other device

bench: keep out of a game

draft: when teams take turns choosing new players

dyslexia: a condition in which a person usually faces extra challenges in reading, spelling, and writing

forward: a player who usually plays near the basket

franchise player: the best player on a team now and in the future

off-season: when a sports league is inactive

podcast: a music or talk show available to download from the internet

pro: short for professional, taking part in an activity to make money

rebound: grabbing and controlling the ball after a missed shot

rookie: a first-year player

turnover: losing possession of the ball to the opposing team

Source Notes

7 Marc J. Spears, "WNBA Star A'ja Wilson Is Ready to Take on the World for Team USA," Undefeated, February 6, 2020, https://theundefeated.com/features/wnba-star-aja-wilson-is-ready-to-take-on-the-world-for-team-usa/.

11 Dorothy J. Gentry, "A'ja Wilson Was Benched in College. Now She's an MVP," FiveThirtyEight, September 22, 2020, https://fivethirtyeight.com/features/how-aja-wilson-fulfilled-her-promise/.

15 Gentry.

20 Spears, "WNBA Star A'ja Wilson."

25 Mike Uva, "Competition at Home Fueling A'ja Wilson for Start of New WNBA Season," WACH FOX57, May 24, 2020, https://wach.com/sports/usc-gamecocks/competition-at-home-fuleing-aja-wilson-for-start-of-new-wnba-season.

Learn More

A'ja Wilson Foundation
https://www.ajawilsonfoundation.org

A'ja Wilson—WNBA
https://www.wnba.com/player/aja-wilson/

Doeden, Matt. *G.O.A.T. Women's Basketball Teams*. Minneapolis: Lerner Publications, 2021.

Kelley, K. C. *WNBA Young Stars*. Mankato, MN: Child's World, 2020.

Scheff, Matt. *NBA and WNBA Finals: Basketball's Biggest Playoffs*. Minneapolis: Lerner Publications, 2021.

Women's Basketball Hall of Fame
https://www.wbhof.com

Index

A'ja Wilson Foundation, 5, 22

COVID-19, 17, 24–27

high school, 10, 13, 22

injuries, 16–18

Las Vegas Aces, 4–6, 14, 26

Mountain Dew, 23

Olympic Games, 27

Shaanxi Red Wolves, 15–16
Social Justice Council, 21
Staley, Dawn, 11, 15

University of South Carolina, 11, 13

WNBA Draft, 5, 13–14
WNBA Finals, 5, 26

Photo Acknowledgments

Image credits: Sam Wasson/Getty Images, pp. 4–5; Ethan Miller/Getty Images, p. 6; AP Photo/Julie Jacobson, pp. 8, 14; AP Photo/The Sun News, Janet Blackmon Morgan, p. 9; Tracy Glantz/The State/MCT/Alamy Stock Photo, p. 10; AP Photo/Gary McCullough, p. 11; AP Photo/Scott Kinser/CSM, p. 12; AP Photo/Tim Gangloff/CSM, p. 13; AP Photo/Stacy Bengs, p. 15; Imaginechina Limited/Alamy Stock Photo, p. 16; AP Photo/John Byrum/Icon Sportswire, p. 17; ArtRoms/Shutterstock.com, p. 18; Ethan Miller/Getty Images, p. 19; AP Photo/Phelan M. Ebenhack, p. 20; AP Photo/Mark Lennihan, p. 21; AP Photo/Tom Sherlin/The Daily Times, p. 22; Alexander Tamargo/MTN DEW ICE/Getty Images, p. 23; AP Photo/Wade Payne, pp. 24, 27; AP Photo/Kendall Warner/The News & Advance, p. 25; AP Photo/Phelan M. Ebenhack, p. 26.

Cover image: photographer/agency/Getty Images.